THIS
STRANGEST
EVERYTHING

7-17-68

Also by John Ciardi

AS IF (1955)

I MARRY YOU (1958)

39 POEMS (1959)

IN THE STONEWORKS (1961)

IN FACT (1962)

PERSON TO PERSON (1965)

THIS
STRANGEST
EVERYTHING

JOHN CIARDI

Rutgers University Press
New Brunswick, New Jersey

Some of the poems in this volume were first published
in The Atlantic, Ladies Home Journal, Literary Magazine of Tufts
University, The New Yorker, The Saturday Review.

Printed in the United States of America by
H. Wolff, New York.

For
Leonard and Gertrude,
souls and graces

Contents

THE LONGEST WAY IS BACK

Sunset and after 3
The longest way is back 4
Talking myself to sleep at one more Hilton 6
Back through the looking glass to this side 9
Daemons 11
At my father's grave 13
Coming home on the 5:22 14
Letter to a midnight 18
Was a man 21
Epithalamium at St. Michael's cemetery 24
Incident 26
Boy 28
Small elegy 30
A crow's long scratch of sound 34
One day 36
An edge, a twilight, a plover 37
The catalpa 38

A BLACK-BREAD STORE

Why don't you write for me? 41
A ballad of teleologies 43
Two lectures and a few flourishes 46
Galileo and the laws 50
Some sort of game 52
Crystal night 54
The formalities 56
Notes on the psalmist 59
New Year's Eve 61

Fragment 64
Tommy's pond 65
The week that was 66
Project for a cliff-face 67
Advertisement for a reader 68
A magus 69
After a night that came to nothing 71

PENCIL STUB JOURNALS

On the poet as a damned poor thing 75
To Somatica to say nothing, and not "no" 78
On the poet as a marionette 80
For a Schnorrer who is also my friend, within limits 81
Twice, away from Jack, I thought of him 82
L'Inglese 83
Dinner in Chinatown 86
The damned 87
Sermon notes 88
An evening of the private eye 89
To a plinking of mandolins 91
A masque for Buckingham 92
Pencil stub journals 95
On the third planet from the sun 103

THE
LONGEST WAY
IS BACK

Sunset and after

This easy-gone world now—that one cloud it sets to
    like a whale in an aquarium of Chablis
    shoaled on pink niblets. What is it like to be
like nothing? It is like fact, I think. Days go

and the sky invents itself. Sometimes a fête
    dances through it. Sometimes a too-muchness
    of bad watercolors. Sometimes no riches,
good or bad, but crags, stone-waste, a fiat

of that cobalt indifference all worlds are edged by.
    What is it like to see what is? these changes
    of impossible fact? This strangest
everything was here. And gone now. And I

am the hard-come night's man long to dark
    and simpler than God made me. Could
    he make, who is Himself, I think, made
by what is like nothing and leaves no mark.

The longest way is back

The longest way is back. Lazarus learned.
And every grown son at his equinox
among the mating birds will. Day returned
is longer than day gone. The box
of every funeral is glacier slow,
and grounds on fern. The stillest hour's all snow,

but even then sleds burst by in a view
of racing hills. A mother is so small
a taw could be her grave and headstone, too.
A son's a box of lost taws. Is a doll
a daughter's leavings? As the day returns,
the lost doll spills its stuffing in the ferns.

Birds make their nests of it. They come and go
as if all hours were first. The grown son sees
the blur they were ago, ago, ago.
But has a plane to get to. His valise
packs him to what he does. It takes his hand
and pulls him to his taxi. Shall he stand

against that tug? Birds are so light so fast:
how can they pull so hard against that weight,
who could not lift a taw? How do they last

out of all boyhood? It grows late
is less time than it takes a man to pack
and leave again. The longest way is back.

Talking myself to sleep at one more Hilton

I have a country but no town.
Home ran away from me. My trees
ripped up their white roots and lay down.
Bulldozers cut my lawn. All these
are data toward some sentiment
like money: God knows where it went.

There was a house as sure as time.
Sure as my father's name and grave.
Sure as trees for me to climb.
Sure as behave and misbehave.
Sure as lamb stew. Sure as sin.
As warts. As games. As a scraped shin.

There was a house, a chicken run,
a garden, guilt, a rocking chair.
I had six dogs and every one
was killed in traffic. I knew where
their bones were once. Now I'm not sure.
Roses used them for manure.

There was a house early and late.
One day there came an overpass.
It snatched the stew right off my plate.

It snatched the plate. A whiff of gas
blew up the house like a freak wind.
I wonder if I really mind.

My father died. My father's house
fell out of any real estate.
My dogs lie buried where time was
when time still flowed, where now a slate
stiff river loops, called Exit Nine.
Why should I mind? It isn't mine.

I have the way I think I live.
The doors of my expense account
open like arms when I arrive.
There is no cloud I cannot mount
and sip good bourbon as I ride.
My father's house is Hilton-wide.

What are old dog bones? Were my trees
still standing would I really care?
What's the right name for this disease
of wishing they might still be there
if I went back, though I will not
and never meant to?—Smash the pot,

knock in the windows, blow the doors.
I am not and mean not to be
what I was once. I have two shores
five hours apart, soon to be three.
And home is anywhere between.
Sure as the airport limousine,

sure as credit, sure as a drink,
as the best steak you ever had,
as thinking—when there's time to think—
it's good enough. At least not bad.
Better than dog bones and lamb stew.
It does. Or it will have to do.

Back through the looking glass to this side

Yesterday, in a big market, I made seven thousand dollars
while I was flying to Dallas to speak to some lunch group
and back for a nightcap with my wife. A man from Dallas
sat by me both ways, the first from Campbell's Soup,
the other from some labeled can of his own, mostly water,
and Goldwater at that. Capt. J. J. Slaughter

of United Airlines kept us all in smooth air and well
and insistently informed of our progress. Miss G. Klaus
brought us bourbon on ice, and snacks. At the hotel
the lunch grouped and the group lunched. I was,
if I may say so, perceptive, eloquent, sincere.
Then back to the airport with seventeen minutes to spare.

Capt. T. V. Ringo took over with Miss P. Simbus
and that Goldwater oaf. We made it to Newark at nine
plus a few minutes lost in skirting cumulo-nimbus
in our descent at the Maryland-Delaware line.
"Ticker runs late," said the horoscope page. "New highs
posted on a broad front."—So the good guys

had won again! Fat, complacent, a check
for more than my father's estate in my inside pocket,
with the launched group's thanks for a good day's work,

I found my car in the lot and poked it
into the lunatic aisles of U.S. 1,
a good guy coming home, the long day done.

Daemons

I pass enough savages on the street
to credit the daemon in things. But they
have forgotten how the soul breathes
from plant, beast, and man and must
be propitiated. They do avoid thirteenths,
walk wide of ladders and black cats,
make the sign of the cross for hearses.
But shabbily. Ritualists without conviction.

My mother, at bone and breath, was the savage
I learned from. When we poured
concrete for a new house, she leaned over
the half-filled forms muttering,
and dropped in a penny, a crucifix, a key,
then pricked her finger and shook out
a drop of blood. Then stood there,
waiting. Giving, had she given enough?

Because she meant to take no chances,
I thumbed a bean pod open and gave her
the beans, saying nothing, and she threw those
in. That started her going again. Off
she went to her kitchen and brought back

oil, wine, a sliver of meat, snippets
of all the food we had. In they went. Then
she thought a minute and told me to spit.

She was using everything she knew anything
about, and she knew she was using it. That
is my kind of savage. She was living at
the ghost of all she lived by.
Now suppose I say again I do
credit daemons? Suppose I pick up
a conch and blow it and ask if it hears
itself making music?—the idea loses you.

But there go the savages in and out of
Tiffany's, the Waldorf, the Cathedral,
the Subway. They take place; they do not
know themselves. They do, I suppose, move
to the music they think they hear. But
what I mean is—you have to hear your self
making the music you didn't know was
in you, living at what you live by.

At my father's grave

A leaf is not too little. A world may rest
in no more shade than spider's weave. Defend
the nit on every underside. I roost
on less than it, and I must yet be found
by the same bird that found St. Francis dead.
It's cold as nothing in the eye I see,
and anything's a wrap. Had I the deed
to all these stones, I'd burn it. Could I say
what world this is and, saying, let it be,
I'd keep as still as wormholes in a thought
and let it lack. A leaf could not blow by
my silence and find room to land. If that
is no real kindness for what sun I had
when I was warm, most kindness is a waste,
all kindness is too little. In my head
there are more teeth than mercies. I'll go west
and set the sun forever when I dare
disturb the leaf that's wedged against my door.

A prosperous well-tailored plump
middle-aged man swings off the train
before it stops. His two-foot jump
and small quickstep spring a small pain
in his hip socket, but his stride
jaunts him away. This is a matter of pride.

—I really did that rather well.
Not a track record, to be sure,
but rather nimble all in all.
—The deft man lets his stride out, feels the power
of blurring past the cracks in the concrete
his shadow strafes. Passionate. An athlete.

—How did this fat and foolish man
come over me? He is not I.
Yet I am he, though I began
as something else. When did I die?
Well, tell the truth: not I but they.
All those I tried in prayer or play,

like trying on a self. Not quite like thought.
Like hope, like fear—no, not like fear:
that's something else. I'm not

afraid of what I am. I can still hear
all I've said. I can see all I've been
—forgiven. Sod rest ye, gentlemen,

let nothing ye dismay. And, above sod,
the world's for trying till the world be seen.
—I used to say this sort of thing to God.
He didn't like an idiot for a son.
I wasn't pleased myself, so I changed style.
I was a little everything for a while.

The one thing I was not until it came
upon me without being asked was this
middle of nothing much with no known name,
this flab of putty playing spry, this piss
out of a tree of apes, this vintage-sour
trying to act like God's first April shower.

—The rest I've been. That ape up in the tree.
The botanist below it. The moon boy
at every bodice. The missionary bee
sucking for souls. The gunner with his toy.
The stink of small ambitions. Party clown.
Professor Poop, pride of the noumenon.

—How many faces I have shed!
I think I see bone! A sharp pencil could
draw out that center till a man is dead,
the fallen pencil pointless as dead wood
when no hand holds it. Yet, in that hand's hold,
the fact and instrument of a man told.

Told from himself to what a God might see
had he a man's eye for the passioning
and stroke and make of what it is to be
too brief for his own fashioning,
yet long enough to shed and shed and shed
what he is not, till he draw his own head.

Draw it to bone if bone is all that stays
into his look. But draw it. Bone of man.
The intricate sad skull, its hollow grays,
the blackened grin, the rounded white brainpan
dove-jointed to the light, the eye's hoar caves
where suns rose and the main deep spent its waves;

held to the light on which the pencil slashed
the drawing home, and made a thing to see
this joker jaunting by, his belly cached

in tailored money, one hip and one knee
creaking on calcium grit through which he plays
Lard Agonistes, muscle man of days.

—Well, I forgive him. Every face melts off
the ape there was and is in every bone.
I know him well enough. I cough his cough
and ache his aches. Closer than mother and son
I bear him and am borne. Like you, and you—
nothing, until a birth pain lets us through.

Letter to a midnight

You will tire of many acceptances. Some of each day
  like money not really worth making will encumber prudence,
  taking time from you without changing it to anything.

The cat, having been fed, will sleep at its own distance
  from sentiment. The clock will auction all houses
  past midnight, hammering home, minute by minute,
  what you can no longer bid for. When the floor creaks
  that is not time but the heat rising. Far off,
  if you listen, you will hear the furnace roaring
  what you paid for. The children are away
  and their return will be only to visit. In her bed
  their mother sleeps, a bride again. Possibly yours.
  But not often. You did not return often enough
  and cannot return. It is yesterday there too long.

Where is the flower from the lapel of a love ago?
  Duty is not enough husband and no father.
  A lost romp is forever. Can you tell them this, kindly?
  No: midnight's a dry correspondent, and stuffy.
  Its letter full of *indeeds*. A harumpher
  of dead and buried *I told you so*'s. I am damned
  to these conversations with an obstinate comfort.
  What a successful house not to live in!

"Bride," I try writing, "come dancing. Business is over;
    all customers dead or asleep. Children, come tumbling,
    screaming, smashing the knickknacks. Disturb me.
    Don't shush them, darling: these papers are better unread:
    tomorrow's market will kiss nothing." To whom
    could I mail it? There is no delivery there. It returns
    addressee unknown. USE ZIP CODE FOR FASTER SERVICE.

"TJ," I try again, "I hope this memo
    will come as no surprise . . . that time of life . . .
    these many years . . . and still the cat I feed
    sleeping across the room its distance from me . . .
    I shall, of course, stay on till the right man . . .
    meanwhile to state my intentions. . . ." A first draft.
    A purpose to sleep on when I learn to sleep.
    Once I have read the books I meant to read,
    permitting interruption, begging impromptus.
    To come into a spending time unspent. . . .

You, too, will tire of doing what is not done
    but only balanced forever because it tips
    forever. Is less than a cat knows, keeping
    to itself. Cannot be ended but only left.
    Another will come, but not to write this letter. That
    you must do for yourself. And the answer, too.

19

Taking both sides of no correspondence to say
what you know is nothing. *I want a first again.*
. . . As if I could know it before I saw it leave. . . .

Was a man

Ted Roethke was a tearing man,
   a slam-bang wham-damn tantrum O
from Saginaw in Michigan
   where the ladies sneeze at ten below
but any man that's half a man
   can keep a sweat up till the freeze
   gets down to ninety-nine degrees.
   For the hair on their chests it hangs down to their knees
     in Saginaw, in Michigan.

Ted Roethke was a drinking man,
   a brandy and a bubbly O.
He wore a roll of fat that ran
   six times around his belly O,
then tucked back in where it began.
   And every ounce of every pound
   of that great lard was built around
   the very best hooch that could be found
     in Saginaw, in Michigan.

Ted Roethke was an ath-a-lete.
   (So it's pronounced in Michigan.)
He played to win and was hard to beat.
   And he'd scream like an orangutan
and claw the air and stamp his feet

at every shot he couldn't make
and every point he couldn't take.
And when he lost he'd hold a wake,
    or damn you for a cheat.

Sometimes he was a friend of mine
    with the empties on the floor O.
And, God, it's fun to be feeling fine
    and to pour and pour and pour O.
But just to show we were not swine
    we kept a clock that was stopped at ten,
    and never started before then.
    And just to prove we were gentlemen
        we quit when it got to nine.

Ted Roethke was a roaring man,
    a ring-tailed whing-ding yippee O.
He could outyell all Michigan
    and half the Mississippi O.
But once he sat still and began
    to listen for the lifting word,
    it hovered round him like a bird.
    And oh, sweet Christ, the things he heard
        in Saginaw, in Michigan!

Now Roethke's dead. If there's a man,
   a waking lost and wanting O,
in Saginaw, in Michigan,
   he could hear all his haunting O
in the same wind where it began
   the terrors it could not outface,
   but found the words of, and by grace
   of what words are, found time and place
    in Saginaw, in Michigan.

Epithalamium at St. Michael's cemetery

My father lay fifty years in St. Michael's bed
till we laid back the covers and bundled in
the hag end of his lost bride, her wits shed
some years before her light. O, bones, begin
with one gold-banded bone. The bride is dressed
in tissue, ten claws folded on no breast.

Man and woman made he them, but gave
dominion to Dominion. Does He know
how deep the whale goes to its grave,
its hull of ribs still trembling in the flow
under the dark he makes there, or that is
unmade? If every deep is His,

then all bounds are abysses, as they were
when the set eyes of Sphinxes still stared through
their gilded doors to a green delta's stir
of rayed and hovering dynasts, while the Jew,
back at his interrupted captivity
in the ashes of lamentation, sang "Eli! Eli!"

What loss is this when nothing's left to lose?
She waited and she came, and he is there,
whether or not he waited. Can we choose

what we shall wait for? Can I find a tear
for what this is? I have none left. I see
a twice unfinished bridal. The chivaree

has been rescheduled. The Capuchin suite—
a grotto off the Via Veneto—
has been reserved for this first night, complete
with its two skeletal cupids flying low.
A crypt of the dead sea. There, side by side,
the sodden groom, the driftwood bride,

begin again forever what they began
in God's will, or the sand-blast through no door,
or the wind in the Jew's ashes, or as this man
and woman crossed their sea once, through whose floor
Capuchin birds silt into the abyss
He sets His bounds by. Or that simply is.

Incident

Not that it matters, or not much, and not
to the children now, but it was
Spring as a daisy chain and not yet hot
but skin-prickle new and the grass
all lazy-breeze lolly when
the madman came up from his wrong roots
and played horrors with the children
who had been playing all sorts
of nothing really, or all, and who died
so hard even one of the cops cried.

Who, for that matter, has cried enough
for what feeds madness? This
small boy and this small girl unwove
their daisies and did not miss
what they had been loving, or just being glad in,
which must be the same thing.
It could have been rock-Winter and no garden.
It did happen to be Spring.
But Spring came to Dachau, too, and not one
corpse there chose his season.

This is a note on stagecraft. Soft days
darken most. Imagination
seizes contrasts. Horror dies

of horror. This could have been done
in a bitter time. Still the soft moon
most calls the wolf; bright sky, the hawk.
Madness wakens beyond intention,
buzzes to soft airs, goes for a walk,
and finds children playing. We are all
dangerous till our fears grow thoughtful.

No death is an invention. They were small bright,
are hugely dark, and everything does matter,
yes, but not to them now. Do stones see light?
winds keep diaries?—a leaf, a child, tatter;
a cause flows. There are
madmen, but horror must first be made.
The cop dried his eyes and swore war,
his tears instantly wasted. Three dogs bayed.
The madman was shot running over the same flowers
the children had dropped. His. Ours.

Boy

He is in his room sulked shut. The small
pouts of his face clenched. His tears
as close to holy water as I recall
any first font shining. A boy, and fierce
in his sacrament, father-forced this two-
faced way love has. And I, who

am chain-chafed and galled as any son,
his jailor: my will, his cell;
his hot eyes, mine. "Whose will be done?"
I think, wrong as a man. —Oh, very well:
I make too much of nothing much. My
will a while. A boy's tears dry

into the smudge of any jam. Time hurts,
but I am not much destiny. I am,
at best, what cries with him; at worst,
a smallest God, the keeper of one lamb
that must be made to follow. —Where?
That takes more God than I am to make clear.

I'm wrong as a man is. But right as love,
and father of the man whose tears I bless
in this bud boy. May he have cried enough

when he has cried this little. I confess
I don't know my own reasons or own way.
May sons forgive the fathers they obey.

Small elegy

I saw a bird pasted to muck.
His death, already part of it,
was half a clod and half a shuck.
Still feathered, but as far from flight
as luck can drag down any wing.
As far as time drags everything.

It is, perhaps, a trifling mood
that solemnizes by small death.
It lay beside a country road,
And I was strolling out such health
as I have not yet quite destroyed
enjoying the diet I have enjoyed.

It was—had been—I still could see
by one small flaunt not yet put by
a red-winged blackbird. Obviously
not much to lose from a whole sky
that, for that matter, once outsoared,
barely begins the mass of God.

—Could I, that is, believe such mass
describes itself to fear or love.
I strolled the only road there was

and guessed a law: there is enough
wayside for every sparrow's fall.
And time enough for all of all.

A bird must be a heavy cause
to change to mud. A man must be
a heavier yet. Then what's that mass
all cause falls to? I think I see!—
How intricate is the world we live!
How simple is the world we leave!

Think it and change! Oh, could I think
this bird back to its weightlessness!
Or that bird, soul! Then I could thank
my father for a massive guess.
And, myself lightened into flight,
soar to some singing Infinite.

Well, then, it is a trifling mood
that solemnizes by small death.
But where's a larger? Have Popes made
their way into a greater earth
than this fluff comes to? All death's small,
into whatever mass we fall.

How large is life? Once on a shelf
a candle lit a plaster saint
and I knelt in a blaze of self.
The reek of guilt would leave me faint
where my mad mother stretched my soul.
Let this bird have the beads I told.

Is it my failure or my luck
that, since then, I have found no death
I could not pause by for a look
and then stroll on—above, beneath,
within this mass that we, outrun,
fall from and to, barely begun?

Have I lost most by wanting less?
I have not happened anywhere
on more regret than I could lose,
nor on more love than I could bear,
nor on more pity than I could give
the small sad days to which we live.

As small as this unfeathering clod
in country muck. Which, who shall mark?
I'd like a mass I could call God.

—I'd like a cruise on Noah's ark:
imagine being there to see
the lives from which all life would be!—

I'm here instead to see one fluff
weighed down into the mass there is.
Any stroll is long enough
to stop a man by elegies
so small they almost lack a cause,
yet leave him guessing out first laws.

A crow's long scratch of sound

A crow's long scratch of sound
begins this valley's day.
Small mists still browse the ground
but slowly thin away
like some white dream of herds
a dream of God once knew.
Now shine the quicker birds.
And now whole greens shine through

where only boulders hump—
a black herd scattered wide
out of the glacial dump.
These dreams shift like a tide.
The crow's scratch hangs up there,
then heals itself away
to a last echoing air
one dream behind the day.

I think this world began
with a somnambulist
who dreamed he was a man,
the husband of a mist,
the father of a thought.

His name may be that sound
whose scratch heals. Or does not.
If echo can be found,

he will be found, twice heard.
Meanwhile, I am a man
awakened by a bird.
Wherever this began,
I'm brother to its change,
son of its stay.
And—on whatever grange—
the beast that feeds on day.

One day

One day in a rush of dogwood all the world married.
There were the flower girls balancing all their airs
like leaf buds on new wood. There was the catered lawn
served in such light as only jonquils candle.
And the mother of all in the cloudhead of her boughs.
Oh, even the father stones were garlanded light.
While the groom at his gap in the hedge stood dark and new,
rain-gloss in the swirls of his bark, and an aspen air
trembling inside him. And nodding and nodding and nodding,
the iris and tulip and hyacinth borders touched heads
in the spray of a last, light-bursting, tiniest, almost
not-rain. And then—so fast it happened there was not time
for reason to change anything dark—the sun,
like all the brass in the orchestra, spoke one note long
to the spray that instantly rainbowed, and there,
down the aisle of its hour, the garden of all was coming.

An edge, a twilight, a plover

I had left myself on the beach like a towel
while no-mind's glaze floated to wherever
zenith is from here. When I got back, my soul
was blue curds; and I, half covered
with the sand everyone else had gone from.
I rolled over and saw seaward a sky striped
blue and white, like a tent, but more a dome
with no center than a place kingpinned and capped.
Not something but part of it. I was still nowhere
but less amply. There was a sea in it. And light
going, though slowly yet. Then a plover lit there,
almost at eye level, gathered its instinct right
for a last jab at the sand and brought up a worm
that hung like an omega from its beak
an instant, then gone. This nowhere from
my eye was edible! I, too, could seek
and find, perhaps. Perhaps not as far
as any bird comes from. Perhaps near. Or here.

The catalpa

The catalpa's white week is ending there
in its corner of my yard. It has its arms full
of its own flowering now, but the least air
spins off a petal and a breeze lets fall
whole coronations. There is not much more
of what this is. Is every gladness quick?
That tree's a nuisance, really. Long before
the summer's out, its beans, long as a stick,
will start to shed. And every year one limb
cracks without falling off and hangs there dead
till I get up and risk my neck to trim
what it knows how to lose but not to shed.
I keep it only for this one white pass.
The end of June's its garden; July, its Fall;
all else, the world remembering what it was
in the seven days of its visible miracle.

What should I keep if averages were all?

A
BLACK-BREAD
STORE

Why don't you write for me?

For you, or of you? It can't be
both. If you must ask that
question, you are not ready for
yourself. If I write for
you, I must write about someone
else: someone dead, though you
haven't heard of that death. If of
you, you haven't heard that
news either. Then what can I tell you?

You see there are few customers
in this business. Not that it matters.
I live by eating up the profits.
There is that to be said for it as
a business: check the books any way
you like; there is always a profit,
and it can always be eaten. . . . Scorn
you? Never. Customers are
always welcome. Cherished even.

I mean I have learned to stock
only what I can live by
when no customers come. When one
does come, therefore, it follows
that he can buy only what I have my

own appetite for. A black-bread
store, if you like. Stiff crusts and
garlicky cores. But learn to like it
and nothing can feed you better.

A ballad of teleologies

Says ego's ape, shaking its tree,
"I'd know exactly how to be,
had I the courage for it, free."

Says Ethelred the Adolescent,
"Strike for the shore! It's manly pleasant
to terrify the southern peasant!"

Says Bonifacio of the Lord,
"Logos, the all-creating Word
that proves Itself is *my* reward!"

Says Teleos the Microscope,
"Look in! This dark through which we grope
is lit by particles of hope!"

Says Father Malthus, "I'm delayed
but not denied. The table's laid
for the last tuber, I'm afraid."

Says Father Marx, who gave the Law,
"I must confess I'm left in awe:
it comes to more than I foresaw."

—What shall *I* say, except, "Roll on!"
I've bought my house, begotten a son.
Most of what time I had is gone.

The only tree I've left to shake
is my own nervous system. "Quake!"
I whisper to it. —But then I wake.

There *are* some peasants I might raid
to prove I'm afraid of being afraid.
what then?—a billion in foreign aid?

I guess I haven't found the Lord
—whoever lost Him. I grew bored
with praying for future bed and board

especially when—if I'm half right—
I'll probably sleep out all night,
and can't foresee much appetite.

That leaves me Teleos, Malthus, Marx.
They're with me like three Noahs' arks
of goblins riding on the darks

of everybody's drowning void.
And, oh, Good Lord, I left out Freud!
—a slip? Still, what's that anthropoid

I started with if an analysis
doesn't reveal he's what a phallus is,
and what he's shaking's really Alice's

hoped-for participation in
the tree, the tribe, original sin,
or just the particles that spin

genetic crises called The State,
which must at last emasculate
what apes it doesn't emulate,

and so rewrite whatever plot
we shall be part of—if we're not
deleted from that afterthought.

Two lectures and a few flourishes

I. ON PICO DELLA MIRANDOLA

Pico della Mirandola, when he was nineteen,
spoke twenty-two languages. He was then at the court
of Lorenzo de' Medici, the gilded Florentine,
in honor of whom he offered to retort
to any seven hundred questions proposed
by the sages of all nations, and to do so
in the language of the asker. It must be supposed
they could not make it to Florence just then, for Pico
remained untested, as all accounts agree.
The date he set was 1483.

Three years later, to honor his lord and friend,
he compiled from Arabic, Hebrew, and Classic sages
nine hundred theses he would rise to defend
in instant disputation. Alas, the wages
of intellect and vaudeville equally
are spent in travel: the High Inquisition,
twitching its low nose, sniffed out heresy:
Pico abandoned Florence and disquisition
and traveled to other parts for his health's sake.

He had too much at stake, and at the stake,
to stay and argue, though, as you may have guessed,
he felt some slight. Not to himself alone

but to all intellect. Was, in fact, depressed
by what the honest mind must yet atone
of the world's fault. And yet shall merit be
triumphant—for a price.
                    Whoever paid it,
he was absolved in 1493
by the Pope himself (who had been, before he made it,
Rodrigo Lenzuolo Borgia, and who had brought
nothing to office that could not be bought
as he had bought it).
                    Can the man of mind
find propositions here to call him forth
to towering exhortation? Or do we find—
with Savonarola perhaps—that a man's worth
is lessened at the stake?
                    Toward a half hope,
I defend Pico who, though he talked too high,
revised low. Buy from the world. When a Borgia's Pope,
buy from the Borgias. But be prepared to buy.
To buy or burn. Unless, of course, you are
enlightened by being lit, cheered when you char.

(In which case, you may share the glory art is,
and some of my admiration, and all of Sparta's,
but first see, *passim*, "Foxe's Book of Martyrs.")

Now, having thus discoursed on things pertaining
to Pico and to Alessandro Sesto,
to intellect, and to the still remaining
uncertainties every honesty must confess to
between conceived idea and the real seizure
a world becomes when licensed from the bed
that bore, then shook to, Caesar and Lucrezia—

having thus discoursed, though with much unsaid,
let me add to those instances that mind
must weigh like diamonds, these addenda: One:
Caesar and Alessandro, both inclined
to politic poisoning, drank off their own potion
by such an error as lets reason hope
for its renewal, and lets morals grow.
Poisoner, watch the cup. Exit one Pope.
And enter, then, addendum Two: although
Caesar drank the same wine, his strength was such
(combined with antidotes he understood)
he did not die, although he suffered much.
His cure was centered in four posts of wood
set firmly in his chamber floor. Each day
a live bull was led in. Thrown on its back,
one leg lashed to each post, the red beast lay,

a two-foot slit cut in its belly's slack
and its intestines drawn. Into the skin
of the still pulsing beast Caesar was sealed
up to his neck. There in delirium in
the blood bath of the beast, the beast was healed.
Which leaves, as footnote to some history,
an image of the species in its tub,
confounding all such morals as will be
drawn from more blood than mind may hope to scrub,
though mind must work at it or not be mind.
Caesar died, fighting for nothing, not much later.
So to addendum Three: two dead, we find
Lucrezia baffling every explicator
of moral balances by living on,
a duchess, honored, and with no regrets
(at least none showing). —And so ends no sermon
but only fact compiled in three vignettes,
footnoted on three tombs, and filed away
where every bone is mankind demonstrated
and so some piece of truth—if we could say
which truth of what each bone once illustrated.

Galileo and the laws

Galileo thought he saw
the spinning center of the Law
radiating pure equations.
He did, too. But the coruscations
of that center left him blind
to the dark rims of man's mind.

The legal center! How it shone!
But soon the man of laws was gone
into exile with a pack
of legal Jesuits at his back.
So, for eighteen chained years, he
wandered a loose periphery.

Then, by a law outside the Law
Galileo thought he saw,
chance blurred its wheel and he was free:
Cosimo, Grand Duke of Tuscany,
gave him a post, a salary,
the aegis of a Medici.

Back came the center, all ablaze.
In a few months and a few days
this Doctor, safe now from the Pope,

constructed his first telescope.
And there it was! He saw! He saw!
The spinning center of the Law

opened its radiant arms! What then?
He saw beyond but not through men.
Beyond the tower, beyond the Dome,
he saw the eye of Kingdom Come,
its First Equations burning wide
and absolute. Then the Duke died.

A Duke died and a Duke was made.
But there the sky began to fade.
In his old age he knelt and lied
the Law away. Before he died,
Milton called, and wept to find
Galileo had gone blind.

. . .

Blind, but no longer blinded, did
the old man see what his sight hid:
the spinning center of that buzz
that crazes all man is and does
and is no less Law than the Law
Galileo thought he saw?

Some sort of game

Toy-maker Ptolemy
made up a universe.
Nine crystal yo-yos he

spun on one string. It was
something to see it go,
half sad to see it pass.

Why won't the things we do
describe reality?
What if it isn't so?—

Why must there always be
some Galileo there
poking his Q.E.D.

into the spinning air
until the spinners break,
the string hangs scrawled nowhere?

Must it be a mistake
to guess a heaven wrong?
Some sort of heaven-quake

and end of song
roared down that telescope.
Somewhere among

such angels as men hope
are there, but do not know,
a dark began to grope.

So toys and angels go.
Not that it's much to me.
I have been reading Poe

and take this liberty
of bumping into rhyme
touched by some irony

what he set to the chime
of Gothic bing and bong
to knell for time

that proves our pretties wrong
with its damned Q.E.D.
End of whatever song,

if any, this may be.

Crystal night

I told one devil to the end
and found no other. In his place
came day by day, the long bone round
—the race.

Came hunters scarified for God,
their magic twitching in their eyes,
their lances cocked for any blood
not theirs.

Came Pharaohs mounted past the world
but with their whole weight on it still.
In their beginning was the word
—kill.

Came sultans dappled by the rays
of their own rubies. Not quite God,
but gods enough to like God's ways
with blood.

Came monks in their own shadows, vowed
to rack out error, thus to save
the essence God had not allowed
a grave.

Came troopers in their polished meat,
too lucid to have tears to shed.
Came order, ordnance. At its feet
the dead.

Came man, alas, by right and wrong,
by can and will, by Hellgate slammed
his red night through, his long bone round
the damned.

The formalities

On September 2, 1945,
the battleship *Missouri*
flagged like a parade
lay anchored in Tokyo Bay and

the Japanese brass with swords
and the frock-coat detail in
silk toppers briefcases and
horn-rims like wine-bottle bottoms

walked aboard on tightropes
they had stretched inside themselves.
and pushing a separate button
for each part of each bow,

rendered unto Douglas MacArthur
what was MacArthur's, and
what was God's too, MacArthur
ignoring the difference, and in

the skeletal witness of Jonathan
Wainwright come from prison, and of
A. E. Percival, British Army,
wherever *he* had come from,

and of a choir of misc available
native and allied brass in open-collar
suntans assigned by the cameras,
and of the cameras themselves—

still and moving and by flash and
previously arranged floodlighting and
with full sound equipment—the
signatures fell-to and it was

done there on God's deck there
in Tokyo Bay into which I had
watched Hewie splash burning less
than two months before with Doc

dead in the nose and O'Dell
probably blubbering a prayer and
Frankie, poor bastard, blind in his
coop di-dahing no message to Whom

and T.J. waving from the top dome
and Chico and Coxie—whoever if any
they were who wanted their medals
getting them all at last—

which is to say boys at bad luck
in their tribe and wings melting
and the photographer come. And had
fish had time in two months

to pick clean Coxie's little go-to-hell
moustache like the one I shaved off,
and Chico's tattoo and the mole on
Frankie's shin and the scapular from

O'Dell's neck and so for each in (or
out of) himself there under the keel
of the battleship *Missouri* on which
the representatives of the nations

stood witnessing how much like God
Douglas MacArthur was and what a
candidate He would make
if only He were a civilian?

Notes on the psalmist

"What is man?" the Psalmist cried.
"Equal," declared the Declaration.
"Mine," the Manifest State replied,
"I am his relevance and occupation."

What does a man do? I don't know.
I hope he refuses some of every election;
at least the electioneering. Though
I want him to vote, if only by defection.

He comes to nothing. Astronomers, at least,
are sure he will. And wives suspect.
It's easy for a man to be a beast,
hard for him to select

one of whatever he can't have two of.
Hunger is punctual in him. Given some
of anything, he cannot get enough.
When they have most to say, most men are dumb,

then garrulous about nothing. Men are boys
who find out about dying, and then forget.
They do not suffer much: their day annoys
more than it hurts. No one has answered yet

the Psalmist's question. If you thought I would,
you couldn't have been listening. Or you can
hear only what you choose—the aptitude
most like a man.

New Year's Eve

The age is running out. I guess I feel
the established sympathies. Were I Chinese
I could be twice as sure of the Real real.
And twice as wrong. Pass me the bourbon, please.

The age is running on. What can it do
but change into itself? Here's to what goes.
I'm still betting the blue chips to pull through.
That speaks some faith. Though in what, heaven knows.

King has the Nobel. Let his people go.
I wronged them some. But guilt's a luxury
I left with Father Ryan long ago.
Is a blind kitten proof a cat can't see?

Miss Hemens called me "crass" at seventeen.
That poor starched ruffle of the high inane!
Without her damned ideals she might have seen
I was only one part crass to ten insane

from trying to make sense of my own glands
in her wax museum. Well, I learned what to say.
I grabbed the whole hot crockful with both hands
and slopped it to her till I got my A

and even the valedictory. So, to you
from failing hands the flaming torch we throw.
Don't catch the lit end. But in case you do,
for God's sake have the good sense to let go.

I've still got marks where a few blisters were
to prove which end I caught in 'forty-five.
Still, all I really suffered was saying "sir"
to idiots. And I got off alive.

—That's good enough. Who's sorry for the dead
except in editorials and through mikes?
Boys are the cash of war. Whoever said
we're not free-spenders doesn't know our likes.

The government's as good as government
intends to get. What's in our histories
if not the long miscarriage of intent
when good goes public? Pass the bourbon, please.

The age is running out. May it run on:
the error that lasts longest is the right.
Let Truth just keep its hands off the red button,
and that's about as lofty and as bright

as we need ever be to get our A
from Christ, Miss Hemens, or the Eumenides—
whoever does the grading. If on the way
mercies may rain, why then let in all mercies.
It won't be quite a flood for a long day.
Meanwhile it's dry here. Pass the bourbon, please.

Fragment

To the laboratory then I went. What little
right men they were exactly! Magicians
of the micro-second precisely wired
to what they cared to ask no questions of
but such as their computers clicked and hummed.

It was a white-smocked, glass, and lighted Hell.
And their St. Particle the Septic sat
lost in his horn-rimmed thoughts. A gentlest pose.
But in the frame of one lens as I passed
I saw an ogre's eye leap from his face.

Tommy's pond

Frogs' eggs in globular clusters
cloud a jellied universe. A light-bending
Magellanic scum seeded with black lusters.
Has God said this sending?

In the pomegranate of Mother Church, saints
are such seed. Their ruby blood-beat—
cloud-bent, and again in the telling—taints
light as life does. It is no feat

to misunderstand a universe: all man-time
fables great possibility wrong.
Yet seed does burn. Slime
is a sure fire. Its puddle-hung

plenum will burst, these periods
become commas in a heartbeat beyond
pleroma, their myriad myriads
unsaid as galaxies. In any pond.

The week that was

The pet shops were advertising non-rabid bats
for air-raid shelters. ("For that natural touch.")
LBJ and Mao were placing bets.
("The sky's the limit.") Overkill held her torch
high over the harbor. ("Give me your weak, your poor.")
England asked to be mentioned as a world power
and France said, *"Comment?"* (Transmitted as "No comment"
by the wire services, and botched by a lino-hack
to read "Con meant"—at which Parliament
took qualified umbrage until Nelson gets back.)

After that there was no more direct quotation.
It goes better in paraphrase. Evade the question:
you need no answer. And why speak
what's already in the junk mail?—Those bats sold.
And Norman Rockwell did a cover that week
of a boy and his pet hyena, both oddly soiled,
digging up an old sunset by a charred road.
Comment? No comment. This is pure mood.

Project for a cliff-face

Before I die (said the self-riddling
stonecutter) I mean to practice a
whim on a cliff-face, if I can find
an unused extrusion to be the page
for the following text I shall carve
in the pure practice of nothing but
the art and pleasure of my lettering:

THERE WAS A TIME BEFORE MAN.
THERE WILL BE A TIME AFTER.
I SPEAK ONLY WHAT IS EVIDENT.
BUT AS LONG AS THERE REMAINS
ANY MAN WHO CAN READ THESE
WORDS, NONE WILL BELIEVE THEM,
AND AFTER, NO ONE WILL KNOW
WHETHER TO BELIEVE THEM OR NOT.

Advertisement for a reader

This itch to sit at paper and to say
a midnight into fact, a flesh to rhyme,
is what I do instead of doing. May
the life I do not live in the still time
I sit here scratching, by some grace
there is in words, be justified. At best
nothing does better by the untold race
than its own tongues. So have all men been blest
by deeds of words from dead men who took time
they have no longer, but were glad to take
when they were rich, to make into a rhyme
they have forgotten, what they itched to make.

A magus

A missionary from the Mau Mau told me.
   There are spores blowing from space.
   He has himself seen an amazing botany
   springing the crust. Fruit with a bearded face
   that howls at the picker. Mushrooms that bleed.
   A tree of enormous roots that sends no trace
   above ground; not a leaf. And he showed me the seed
   of thorned lettuces that induce
   languages. The Jungle has come loose,
   is changing purpose.
                Nor are the vegetations
   of the new continuum the only sign.
   New eyes have observed the constellations.
   And what does not change when looked at?—coastline?
   sea? sky? The propaganda of the wind reaches.
   Set watches on your gardens. What spring teaches
   seed shall make new verbs. A root is a tongue.

I repeat it as he spoke it. I do not interpret
   what I do not understand. He comes among
   many who have come to us. He speaks and we forget
   and are slow to be reminded. But he does come,
   signs do appear.
              There are poisoned islands far over:
   fish from their reefs come to table and some

glow in the dark not of candlelight. A windhover
chatters in the counters of our polar camps.
A lectern burns. Geese jam the radar. The red phone
rings. Is there an answer? Planes from black ramps
howl to the edge of sound. The unknown
air breaks from them. They crash through.
What time is it in orbit? Israeli teams
report they have found the body, but Easter seems
symbolically secure. Is a fact true?

How many megatons of idea is a man? What island
lies beyond his saying? I have heard, and say
what I heard said and believe. I do not understand.
But I have seen him change water to blood, and call away
the Lion from its Empire. He speaks that tongue.
I have seen white bird and black bird follow him, hung
like one cloud over his head. His hand,
when he wills it, bursts into flame. The white bird
and the black divide and circle it. At his word
they enter the fire and glow like metal. A ray
reaches from him to the top of the air,
and in it the figures of a vision play
these things I believe whose meaning I cannot say.

Then he closes his fist and there is nothing there.

After a night that came to nothing

They're twittering again, my day-starters, and another
    night's paled out of nothing with no
word found certain for it. When does the author
    of nothing sleep? After nothing. In an hour or two.

But what a full first sound everywhere!
    What a city of small bell towers a dawn is
after the round-still pace-swallowing star-stare
    dead desert any crossed night was!

It's a glad gate come to, here, through nothing or
    everything possible. I tried and could not
say even a sorrow, but strewed some world's floor
    with the scrapped paper of a souvenir tommyrot.

Then I heard—one-two-three from a tree—what one hears,
    and a chatter nearby and a coo far away.
Silver-windowed at first till the silvering clears
    and the twittering goes mad in itself. And its day!

PENCIL
STUB
JOURNALS

On the poet as a damned poor thing

I adored her and she giggled and I adored her.

It was entirely summer in her fleshdom
and she her own breeze through it, tittering leaves
that trembled round her bearing. Lemons glowed
on reaches of her tousling. Honeydews
bent light rays round her like a gravity.
She shucked like new corn. Was it to bed or table
she let me spill her, giggling as I nibbled
cherries and flesh of pears and bursting grapes?

I wrote gold reams of nothing that could say
how she lay by me, sleeping as I watched
what Raphael forgot the light could do
when he ran out of angels to stand in it.
Hers was the face of the most stupid angel,
too lost in its own bliss to think of being,
apart from all but its own representation.

That child-head lay adrift above her body
like a small separate soul above the Spheres
of Dante's walk across the universe.
"Beatrice!" I thought nights when I sweated to write her.
But when I crossed at last the swollen Eden
where she stood lit in her gold choruses,

that face of floating heaven knit its brows:
"Alighieri?" it said. "Ah, yes, you're Gemma's husband.
—What's all this you've been writing about me?"

It should have been vision enough to warn off visions,
but pens are hypodermic, and she was the drug
addiction is the dream of. I heard her giggle
floating above us like a face in a cloud,
or blind and separate as a *putta* smirking
from a gilt cornice over a Roman bed
where a boy-cardinal knelt, burning in prayer
to all of her sprawled summer in his arms.

Nothing could save his soul from incoherence.
He swore to make her shudder as he had
for wasting visions, but a vision came:
she was a peach tree, an Ovidian soul
trapped in a golden bearing all might eat
and none might change a leaf of but the wind
that tittered through her. Rising in a rage,
he leaped into her branches to shake down
one fruit of her locked soul. But though he hurled
whole tempests at her, not one gold globe fell. . . .

I was the only windfall in that dream,
a lump among the stubble at her roots,
hearing that other breeze her green sprays toyed with
in their own climate, above the death of mind.

She giggled and I died and still she giggled.

To Somatica to say nothing, and not "no"

Avoid dialogue, Somatica. What you are
is whole orations, but you have nothing to say.

A much-anthologized Egyptian tellurian
who took a first at the University of Babel
and became Professor of Communication Skills
has traced all subsequent incoherence
to social forces behind the umlaut shift.

Dialect, he proposed, is autotelic.
It takes no God to confuse men
from one another and men and women
from one another. What they could not say
in the hypothetical first language
they will not say in polyglot.

He has, moreover, demonstrated
by a cunning osteosynecdoche
that no trace of functional change
has accompanied the evolution of tongues.
It is, therefore, a likely hypothesis
that all bones are as articulate as any.
Language study, he concluded, is pointless
except as a way of multiplying evidence
after the verdict of all ossuaries.

He was an Egyptian and learned beyond clarity,
but a wizened hump of early death.
You are a seeming immortality of amplitudes,
an evident and self-naming garden again,
itself every communication skill.

Can you not learn from a dead Egyptian
who pondered his life away to idea
that the tellurion measures silently
what there are no words for?

I have just returned from his funeral again
and I am sermonized to crapulence.

Must there be a labyrinth in every apple?
A syllabus of motives for every unbuckling?

You are the Eden of all grammar.
Open your gates silently and let me in.
I promise an end to jargon. Like all bones,
I clatter, and have nothing to say.

On the poet as a marionette

A comic in a mashed hat, eating
the strings he dangles by, leaps, and
a wooden prayer is said, beating
its breast like a doorknocker. Its hand
opens and a nail falls out of
the palm. A hinge twitters:
a bird-sung gate of imagined love
admits tenants, but steam fitters
are smashing the pipes because
I crossed their picket line. Help me!
Oh, help me from this trap in the flaws
of no reason who meant only to be
agile, but snagged, and was made to eat
the strings I was strung on.
There is no door where my hands beat
and none to prayer. I am gone
adangle my own beginning, who want
only to unsnarl, to think, to be
not wooden. Perhaps not to recant
love. Or only, possibly,
not to care. Only to be free.

For a Schnorrer who is also my friend, within limits

To deny sympathy is some death, and I have dying enough
to have no taste for more. Flowers of the soul,
flowers of the psyche, flowers of whatever love
is possible after clinical discussion. And if reason's to extol,
reason in mercy. So, by first names, welcome.
And here's food. And three days' bed. And take money to
      leave on.
—But why, with your health to your bones, and no sum
to your day's visible, and your own bride to conceive on—
you yourself having elected poverty—should I,
who loathed the wench from the start—the mother of thirst—
come up with the cash to publish this soul's cry
you won't taint with wages? I'll be damned first.

Twice, away from Jack, I thought of him

Once in snowed-in winter I was caught
on a Utah mountain till a blower plow
slammed head-down through the drifts and shot
a creeping ten-mile howl of rainbow snow.
I followed it down the gap, all roar and light,
until it came to where the road was black,
and it turned around frustrated, its loud bite
still gnashing, empty—and I thought of Jack.

And again in no known season at Waikiki.
I had taken the elevator to the nothingth floor
of the Surfing Hilton for some chivaree
at a pots and pans convention, and the door
slid open on the waterfall roar of Hell
dive-bombing its own turbines while a flak
of gaggle broke in the acoustic shell
of its own carved canyon—and I thought of Jack.

L'Inglese

Walpole, traveling in the Alps,
talked of goat trails and abysses.
Powdered wigs make prickly scalps
in a chaise above a crisis.

"The *least* step"—so he wrote to West,
would have tumbled wig and all
into such fog and sudden rest
that—well, he had no wish to fall.

"But is it possible," he thought,
"the next step is not one too many?"
While the sweating peasants sought
footholds for their daily penny.

One man's terror, one man's trade.
With milord upon their shoulders
and a long way back to bed
the porters edged around the boulders.

Came "a cruel accident."
Next day Walpole still bemoans:
when the trail at last had bent
to an almost-road of stones,

he lets his little spaniel out
("the prettiest, fattest, dearest creature!")
—for its creature-needs, no doubt,
or to admire some Alpine feature.

"When from a wood"—he wept and wrote—
"a young wolf sprang at once and seized
poor, dear Tory by the throat"—
and vanished, one must guess, well pleased.

"I saw it but I screamed in vain!"
—the prey was seized, the wolf was gone.
What seemed, above all else, to pain
Walpole, once the thing was done,

was that it happened in full day—
"but two o'clock and broad sunshine!"
His "Alpine savages"—for pay,
and full, he wrote, of "sour wine"—

made such commotion as seemed due,
but had their Englishman to bear.
In three leagues Turin came in view.
And they could rest once they were there.

Envoi

Sensibility better suits
the man inside the chaise
than the bearers—ugly brutes—
of those Alpine ways.

Yet the weight falls on all mankind
the day the wolf attacks.
Milord had great griefs on his mind;
they, milord upon their backs.

Dinner in Chinatown

Out of a doorway, a halloween black
flitter across the City of New York's lit
bannered calendar of the Year of the Snake,
comes a rag of a face with no eye slit
anything can see through. A briar touches,
not quite scraping, my arm. A breath
I think I can see in air debouches
from a vent in mildew. A death
that's still thirsty whines, "Please, sir,
my need is great." —And the rag does see,
knows it phrase has caught me. From what rafter
has this fallen to rise and outguess me
before I have guessed myself? "Not bread alone,"
it says with a shrug that could be debonair.
"I am an empty cup, sir, and no one
can fill me. Help me to drown where
my thirst is." —And knows the dollar in my hand
as if he put it there. Palms it, as if on cue.
And bows, understanding what we understand.
Not thanks. "May your dinner refresh you,"
he says. No beggar. A commuter from Heaven to Hell.
A salesman who has sold what he came to sell.

The damned

Martyrs, gunmen, angry wives,
desperate husbands, and fugitives
snap their lives with guns and knives,

lions and visions, jolts and jars,
poison, plunges, and gas from cars.
They set their hearts on seeing stars

and they see stars. Through every haze
that's in them all their nights and days
they get to see the whole sky blaze

that once. Just once. But once will do.
Finalities are not to chew.
The damned get one gulp. Then they're through.

We couldn't praise them, you and I.
Still, we note as they plunge by
they do stick to the point. That's why

we half admire them. —I confess
I do. Whatever their distress
they leave with something to express.

We don't die: we just digress.

Sermon notes

It's easy to walk out of Hell. But there
Hell starts again. Another channel but
the same damned show. Hell's what we are, not where.
It's easy to walk out of Hell? To what?
To exactly nothing nowhere and unemployed.
The Anti-Hell's not Heaven but the Void.

An evening of the private eye

"I live, therefore I love," said the Excerpt-Lifter
and Skimmer of Beatitudes, paying no
attention whatever to Plagiary. "Ach, so?"
crouped the Teutonic Monocle, the Brandy Snifter,
and the Iron Cross for Continental Manners,
"I live, therefore I follow Particular Banners."

"Boys," said the Advanced American Female who
had learned her Languages, married Breeding,
and renounced Mere Nakedness for Wider Reading,
"I love, therefore I live." And splitting in two,
she gave her Vowels and Aspirates to the Civilian
and her Consonants to the Thoroughly Charming Villain.

"I live, therefore I live—in some bemusement,"
said the Prosodic Eavesdropper at his Key-Hole
into the Obvious Infinite. "This See-Hole
is good at least for Relative Amusement."
—"Arrest that man!" cried all those Coupling Parts
of Speech, ajabber at their Lively Arts.

"Judgment!" called Monumental Momus. "Hear me!
I pronounce one a Frappé. Two a Bore.
I pronounce three a Particle on No Shore.

I pronounce four Unborn until he fear Me,
Uncock his Eyeballs and Rewrite his Face
in Characters legible to Prevenient Grace."

"Goodbye," said the Private Eye as it Withdrew.
"I leave, therefore you lose." And they were Gone.
Then the First Impulse that he Came Upon
shrugged off Habituation and Away they Flew,
Entasseling every Twig with Lints of Spring,
Inducing Airs, and Summoning Bones to Sing.

To a plinking of mandolins

The Capitoline is rocky
where the heroes, bronze and stone,
stare holes in the sky. *Che sciocchi!*
—they think they're working for Rome!

Maybe even the Romans think so,
wherever the Romans are,
whatever sky they stare through
for a look at the old *città*

(già orbis, ma mai più)
whose heroes, bronze and stone,
have stared the sky clear through
to see where they have gone.

A masque for Buckingham

"Here's to the bodies from which we come.
Here's to Hell and what's south of Rome.
And here's to the stuff that gags us all."
—Said Shadow-and-Spit to sad St. Sprawl
as they leaned on the Blessed Damosel Bar,
as he spat out the butt of a sugared cigar,
as he tossed off a sickening mixture of
grenadined ichor and watered love
served up by Alfred T, Lord God,
who was doing time for writing "Maud."

In came Regina victoriously.
"We are pleased," she said to aforesaid T,
"to ask of Alfred, our good and true,
if he has seen Albert." (She looked right through
Shadow-and-Spit and St. Sprawl, who,
taking their punishment better than men,
gagged the stuff down, said "Again,"
and damned themselves deeper while Alfred Lord
T aforesaid mixed and poured.

The syrup decanted, Alfred T
looked up at her blinking Majesty
and said in a voice like stone on stone,
"Why not leave the poor sot alone?

I've seen him, yes. He has been and gone.
You might try Heaven. It's hard to tell
where they go when they tire of Hell.
Or wait around till things get slack
and he'll show up—they always come back."

"Let her wait outside," said Shadow-and-Spit
and fat St. Sprawl. "The Hell of it
is not, as all the preachers think,
the burning fleas of this damned sink,
nor the sugared emetic we have to drink
from the lady fingers of Alfred T,
but in having to stand here soberly
while all that's sticky and virtuous
comes and goes through the guts of us,

through the shadowy guts we have to fill
with Alfred aforesaid Lord T's swill.
We don't mind the party getting rough,
but no more slumming. This stinking stuff,
we do submit, is bad enough
without her bottomless Majesty
poking her sniff at you and me.
As for Albert, he'll be back or not.
England has many a princely pot

will do as he's told in virtue's name,
yet find himself sick on this very same
saccharine piddle after all
(First Prize at the Exhibition Hall)
because his guts have grown too small
for the roar of scotch or the binge of rye.
Let her wait outside, says I." "And I,"
said Shadow-and-Spit and lame St. Sprawl,
who would rather be damned than not at all.

"We stubbed our souls, but never as much
as her High Victorial Royal Nonesuch,
as His Princeliness of One-Step-Back,
as all the court of the Sniffly Claque,
as Alfred T, their aforesaid hack,
who watered his love with the sticky sweet
blood of Hell for Her Primship's Seat"
—Shadow-and-Spit and the dead Saint cried—
"Till she knows she's damned, let her wait outside."

Pencil stub journals

LONG WEEKEND

Oh, dear, Nan's feeling kittenish. Which of us,
do you suppose, is cast to be the mouse?

AND A LONGER

Lear died of being foolish. Where he lies
what difference would it make had he been wise?

THEREFORE

Why should I learn a better thing to be?
Already, I know better than I do.
Why not forget my character and see
if you can't find another drop or two
of this good liquor. And if you find three,
I'll promise to improve, dear—just for you.

NOT AT HOME

Be damned to the phone. Do you see the crow in that tree?
He wants to say he has come from Plato to me
nonstop with a message he wants me to sit here and guess,
and I think I know what it is, and the answer is yes.

THE VACATIONING PEDANT

I met a pedant at a party in
the Brazen City. He and our host's gin
gave off one air: both mixtures were too thin
but spoiled the air with a vague wish to sin.

ON AN EXALTED NONENTITY

Must we believe that what ascends aspires?
That altitudes are measures of desires?
That nothing mounts until the holy fires
of self have dreamed a height? So Dante taught.
And though it makes some difference who inquires,
and how, this world suggests a counter-thought,
suggested, maybe, by the Prince of Liars,
our Adversary, whose prompting never tires:
the eagle's ticks are airborne but no flyers.

PARENTHOOD

My son was insolent to me.
I blessed him: love is liberty.
My son was insolent to my friend.
I hit him: liberty is to defend.

ON BEING FOUND GUILTY AS CHARGED

Ann says she trusts me, but with such a din
of loving protestation, I begin
to understand she wasn't taken in.

CHOICES

George says he chooses poverty. That's rash.
It's bad enough just learning to live through it.
Name any substitute you like for cash:
I've an experienced aversion to it.

THE TEST

My friend is waiting for me to defend
my actions. Should I try? Have I a friend?

ON AN EXECUTIVE FEMALE

Here is my thought for Miss J. F. MacFee,
Executive Vice-President of Trine, Kull, and Roehm:
*how neatly set the lines of type can be
on sad stiff pages that have missed their poem!*

TO A REVIEWER WHO ADMIRED MY BOOK

Few men in any age have second sight.
But never doubt *your* gift. You are right! You are right!

FOR KARL SHAPIRO ON
THE BOURGEOIS POET

Reason is where first need goes. Chances are
what reason takes. You may be right:
time and our tongue may be too far
from measure for the tick and rote
of metric. Let me doubt it. Let me, too,
admire the gift in anything you do.

AFTER A FIRE

Some of my books were burned. I must
believe at last there is a holy dust.

ON AN ECDYSIAST

She stripped herself of all except pretense.
By nature she and Nature lived to feud
over two words. Her life explains their sense:
born naked into the world, she left it nude.

ON ROMAN TRAFFIC

What is this raging in the streets of Rome?
The poor have all won lotteries and become
by Fiat, Phaetons. Earth and sky, beware!
Zeus, have you one last thunderbolt? Are you there?

THE HARD SELL

The spider in its office of tuned strings
waits at a dream's end for a rumor's twitch.
Manny waits for the phone to ring. It rings.
He pounces and devours the son-of-a-bitch.

FOR CLAVIA ON A REJECTION SLIP

Your soul is full of yearning? So is this prose
you set to tick and rhyme under my nose.

ON EVOLUTION

Pithecanthropus erectus,
could he see us, would reject us.

ON LEAVING THE
INTERNAL REVENUE OFFICE

Why covet this world's goods? The Perfect Man
laid up no treasure on earth. Now no one can.

A VALEDICTORY FOR ROSE

She was to come at nine. I left at ten.
She wrote to scold me: "Why are men
so fretful about time?"
                  God only knows
what I'd been reading—Leigh Hunt, one of those
fine gesturers: I bought one perfect rose,
kept it three days, then sent it. "I suppose,"
I wrote, "because these wither."
                         She replied:
"Your weed has withered, but your Rose has died."

ON MARRIAGE AS AN INSTITUTION

Glori was kind to every cent
she took me for. And am I sorry?
Though Glori and my money went
and I'm back home with Milicent,

my legal sniff and scurry,
my knob-kneed middling unevent,
my meatless Monday curry,
my flannel flitch, with whom I will
live, alas, forever, still
I had my hour of Glori.
What did I get for what I spent?
One line for this damned monument
I shroud in a perpetual Lent:
Meum erat propositum in taberna mori.

ON LEAVING THE PARTY AFTER HAVING BEEN POSSIBLY BRILLIANT FOR CERTAINLY TOO LONG

Where's the magician fast as his own trick?
the balancer as light as what he does
on ropes and air? All curtains fall too quick,
all lights go out too soon. And then what was
magic and weightless must reset its traps,
feed the real rabbit, and take off its tights.
I've had enough bright chippies and old chaps
for any man's collection of brittle nights.
I'm smiled out, talked out, quipped out, socialized
so far from any being, I need the weight

of mortal silences to get realized
back into myself. It's late. It's always late.
It's time I looked back in from outer space
and faced the mirror I still have to face.

On the third planet from the sun

This dream offered itself as if in a movie house.
CAUSES the marquee blinked. I entered,
as if by choice, into the shadows.
Over my head the ray shot the registered

illusion, and something like people almost
loved and died. Bleeding from vials,
heroes recited purposes. In a mist
over them, heroines set the dials

of an emotion, turned it on, turned it off:
THE END. But the house stayed dark
and I did not waken. Someone in love
was sobbing into cotton candy in the back

balcony. A grandmother with slot machine
eyes sat spinning jackpots in her soul.
Addicts in an electric green aura of sin
waited for COMING ATTRACTIONS. The hall

flickered, plunged like an elevator, and grounded.
The elevator door slid open on the precinct house.
The theater manager, mitered and gowned
as a cardinal, pointed a cross

with rechargeable batteries, and two cops in masks
and black tights bent my arms and bound me,
in G.I. uniform, just below the tusks
of her torch, to the Statue of Liberty.

Below me, in the judicial barge, the president,
God the father, the superintendent of schools,
your mother, and a leading columnist
deliberated the evidence of the latest polls

and found me guilty. I agreed it was better so.
I could have awakened myself then.
But was it worth it to explain once more? A sigh
from the Atlantic pinked my high limb with sun.

Morning come bright, as everyday is saved,
married great blue. The church doors of the night
opened, and down enormous organ staves
the day walked out, veiled in the blowing light.

And my last thought was of the world beyond reason
to love. Enduring for it the phantoms
not worth waking from, for fear the risen
day go out with its shadows over the empty tombs.